THOMAS

MAN
IN SPACE
TO THE
MOON

MAN IN SPACE TO THE MOON

FRANKLYN M. BRANLEY

ILLUSTRATED BY
LOUIS S. GLANZMAN

Thomas Y. Crowell Company
New York

BY THE AUTHOR

The Christmas Sky
Experiments in Sky Watching
Man in Space to the Moon
The Mystery of Stonehenge
The Nine Planets

Copyright © 1970 by Franklyn M. Branley

Illustrations copyright © 1970
by Louis S. Glanzman

All rights reserved. Except for use in a review, the reproduction or utilization of this work in any form or by any electronic, mechanical, or other means, now known or hereafter invented, including xerography, photocopying, and recording, and in any information storage and retrieval system is forbidden without the written permission of the publisher. Published simultaneously in Canada by Fitzhenry & Whiteside Limited, Toronto.

Designed by Judie Mills

Manufactured in the United States of America

L.C. Card 79-106567

ISBN 0-690-51685-1
0-690-51686-X (LB)

2 3 4 5 6 7 8 9 10

To

T. E. B.
D. F. B.
K. E. D.

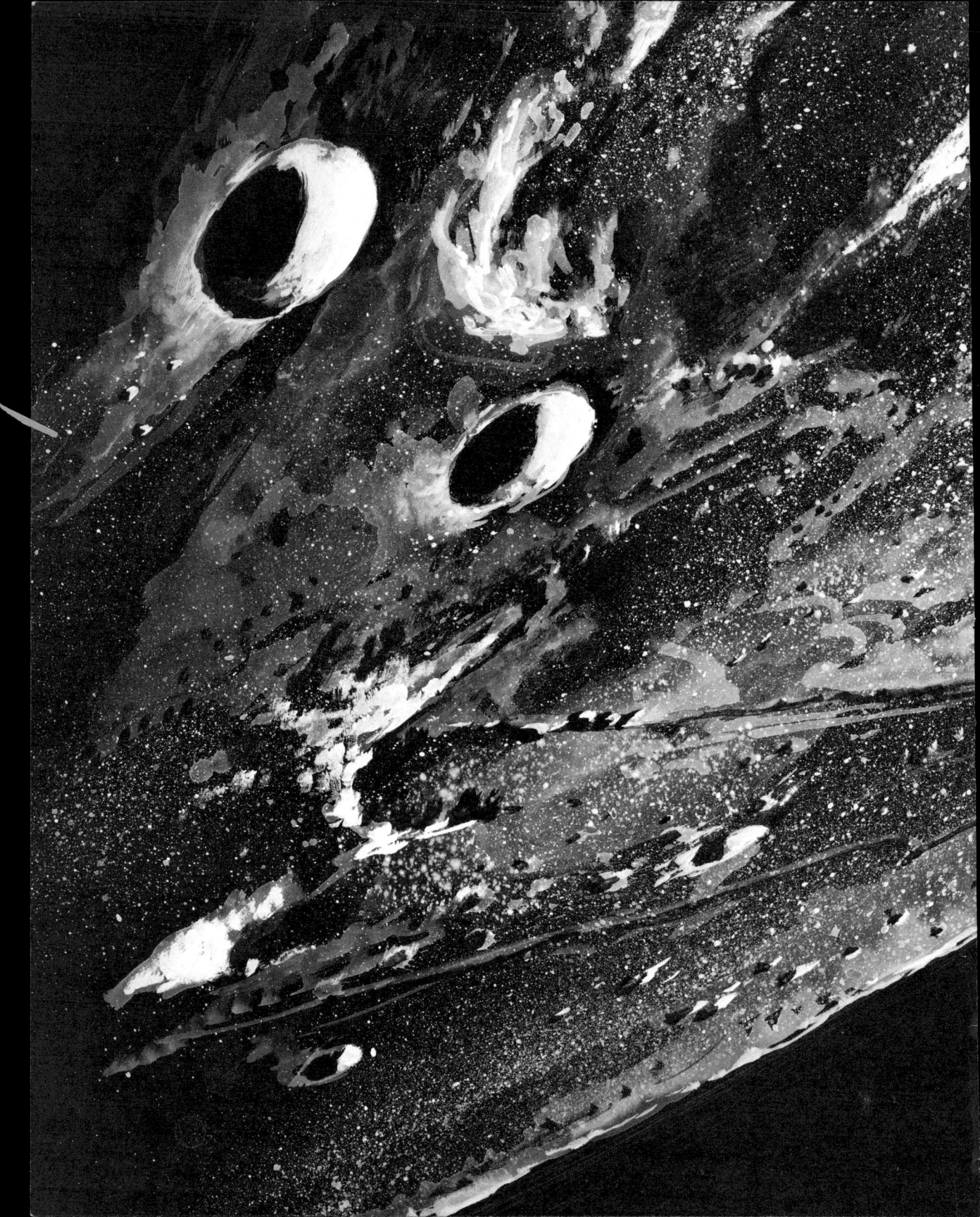

MAN
IN SPACE
TO THE
MOON

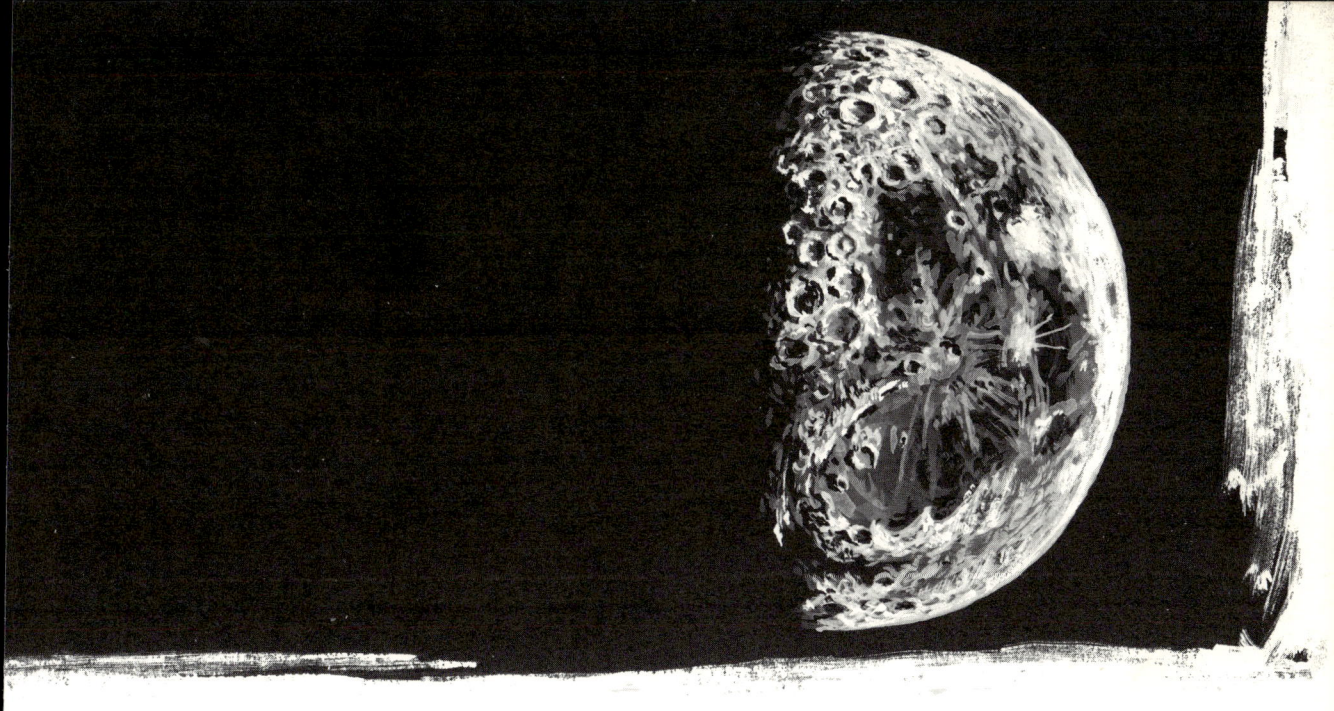

In the summer of 1969, man's age-old dream to set foot on another world was fulfilled. At 10:56:20 (E.D.T.) in the evening of July 20 a man stepped from a spaceship onto the surface of the moon. The man was Astronaut Neil A. Armstrong, commander of the Apollo 11 mission. The space ship was Eagle, a lunar-landing craft. And the ship set down in Tranquillity Base, a limited area in the Sea of Tranquillity (Mare Tranquillitatis, as it was known to men who first named the features of the moon). After a few minutes Armstrong was joined by Edwin E. Aldrin, Jr., the second of three astronauts who were the crew of Apollo 11. The third man, Michael Collins, pilot of the command module, stayed with the mother ship orbiting the moon during the lunar landing. Armstrong and Aldrin were the first men to leave our planet and touch another world. They were the first men to walk upon a lunar "sea," the first to kick their feet through lunar dust. They were the first men to pick up lunar rocks, gravel, and dust, and bring them back to the earth.

The mission that landed men on the moon was called Apollo 11. The flight began four days earlier, at 9:32 A.M. (E.D.T.) on July 16 when the mighty Saturn rocket blasted free of launch pad 39A, a part of the launch complex at Cape Kennedy on the east coast of northern Florida. It took only twelve seconds for the 6,484,280 pounds of fuel, payload, and rocket to clear the tower and to speed on its relentless, determined journey to the moon.

Apollo 11 was part of Project Apollo, a mission that had its beginnings in 1957 when man first succeeded in putting an object into orbit around the

earth. But the story itself has a much earlier beginning. It began a hundred years ago, a thousand years ago, and even before that. It began when ancient man wondered about the moon—what it was, why it changed shape from night to night, why it could not be seen at all on some nights, while at other times it could be seen even in the daytime.

One whole chapter of the story could be filled

just with dreams men have had for reaching the moon. One dreamer said that a cannon sunk in the ground would shoot a ship to the moon. Another said that fabulous birds would carry a straw basket to the moon, a basket in which men sat. Another dreamer believed that a ship could sail to the moon on the wind, much as a sailboat can move across the oceans.

Such ideas were fantasies. Men who thought of them had no understanding of the problems of travel in outer space nor were they concerned about them.

The modern story of a manned journey to the moon is these dreams come true.

It began in 1957. On October 4 of that year the first satellite was put into orbit around the earth. It was called Sputnik 1.

Engineers had learned how to make powerful and reliable rockets. They had learned how to control these rockets hundreds of miles from the earth and how to release satellites at the exact moment needed for them to go into orbit.

After Sputnik 1, other satellites were put into orbit. In a few years hundreds of them had been launched. The orbits of most of the satellites decayed, which means that the satellites came down into the lower atmosphere. As they descended, friction caused them to heat up so much that they changed to white-hot gases. The orbits of some satellites did not decay. Those satellites far from the earth are still in orbit and will continue to be for thousands of years.

Satellites told us a lot about outer space. We measured the amount of dust and radiation in space, the magnetic field of the earth. We mapped the earth and took pictures of the clouds that cover much of the earth most of the time. Other satellites were used to relay television pictures around the world.

Before a satellite is launched scientists equip it with instruments to measure certain conditions or to do certain jobs. If a satellite encounters a condition which no one expected, the satellite cannot gather information about it, because there are no instruments aboard for the purpose.

That's one of the main reasons why men had to be sent into outer space, and to the moon. A man can observe and gather information about expected conditions. But he can also observe and learn something about conditions that are entirely unexpected.

By 1961, four years after the Space Age began, rockets big enough to send a man into orbit had been developed. On April 12, 1961, the Russians launched Vostok 1. Yuri A. Gagarin was the cosmonaut aboard it. He was the first man to go around the earth in a spaceship. This event was the beginning of the Apollo mission, for now men thought seriously about the possibility of sending men to the moon. A year later, on February 20, 1962, the first American went into orbit. He was John H. Glenn, Jr., aboard a Mercury capsule. Glenn

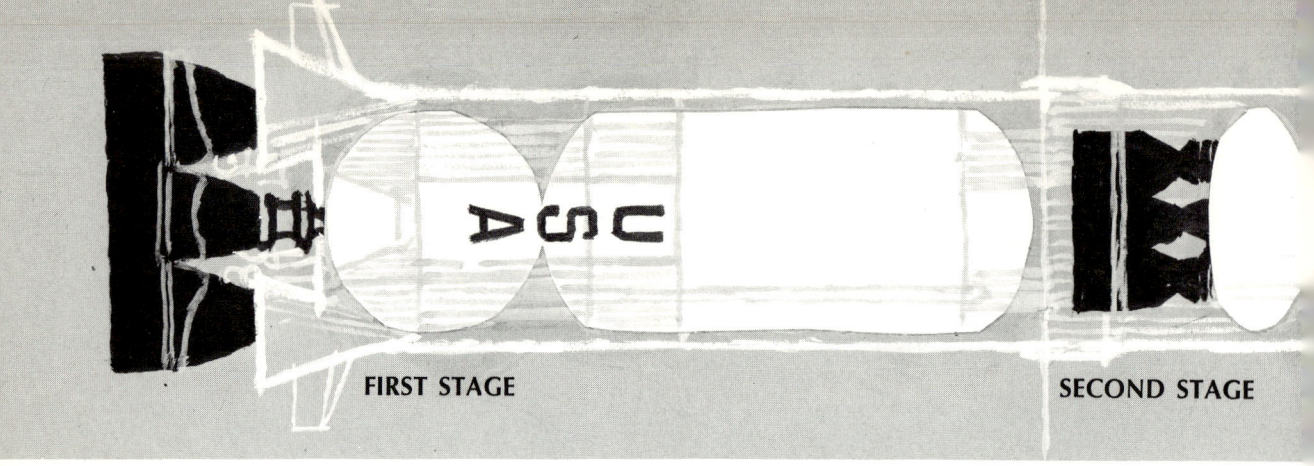

FIRST STAGE   SECOND STAGE

went around the earth three times before re-entry.

Since 1961 more than three dozen men have gone into earth orbit, or on journeys to the moon. And one woman. Her name is Valentina V. Tereshkova. She went around the earth 48 times, beginning her journey June 16, 1963, aboard Vostok 6.

By 1968 we had learned how to put men into outer space, how to keep them alive in their capsules, and how to bring them back to the earth safely. Also, by 1968 the huge Saturn 5 rocket had reached full reliability. Engineers were almost one hundred percent sure that every part of the rocket would work right every time it was fired. The vehicle was ready to push an Apollo command ship into orbit with three men aboard. The Apollo 7 ship was launched October 11, 1968. Every part of the flight was successful. Before re-entry Apollo 7 had gone around the earth 163 times and

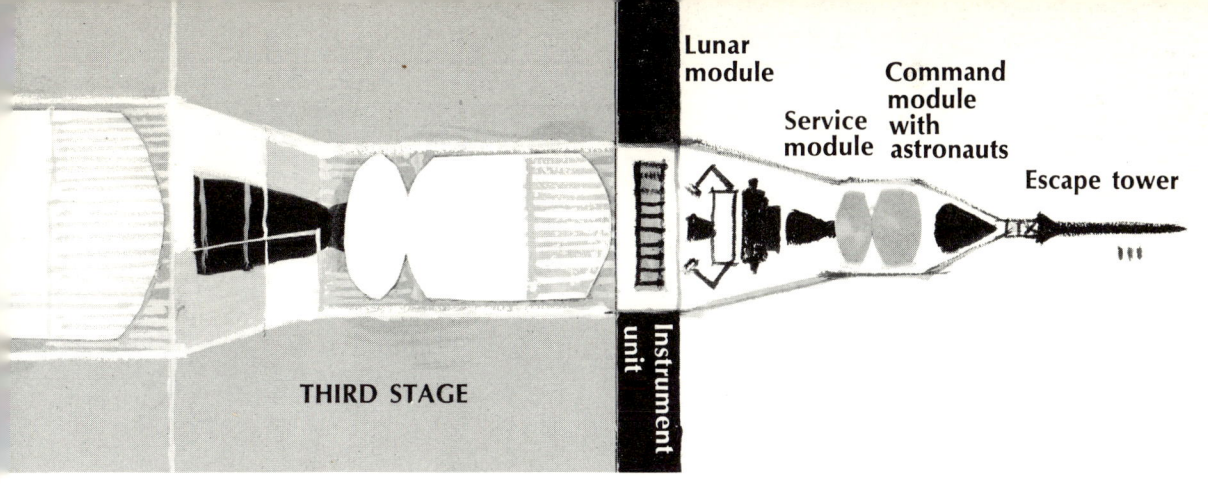

had been in outer space for more than 260 hours.

The Saturn 5 is a three-stage rocket that is 363 feet tall. The first-stage engines fire with a heavy, earth-shaking, thunderous roar. They lift Apollo away from the earth, and then the second engines push it higher. The third-stage engine fires briefly to put the ship into orbit—118 miles above the surface. The two lower stages have been jettisoned. The command and service modules, the part with the men inside, are still fastened to the third-stage engine. It is going about 18,000 miles an hour.

During two circuits of the earth, the entire ship is checked and rechecked. If all is well, the third-stage engine is fired again. The ship reaches 24,000 miles an hour. It is going fast enough to escape earth's gravity, and to journey to the moon.

Apollo coasts to the moon, taking 66 hours to reach it. Slight corrections are made in the orbit by firing small rockets aboard the service module.

Three men are inside the crew compartment. It is a cone-shaped capsule 12 feet long and 13 feet wide. Behind the crew compartment is a service module. It is a cylinder 22 feet long that houses the electrical system, the oxygen supply, a rocket engine for slowing down the vehicle (by firing backward) and for speeding it up when necessary.

During the Apollo 11 mission, the flight to the moon, the astronauts had continuous radio contact with the Manned Spacecraft Center at Houston, Texas. They removed their space helmets and breathed the oxygen inside the vehicle. The men unfastened the belts that held them to their couches, and they moved around. However, movement inside a spaceship is quite different from movement on the earth. A spaceship coasts to the moon. Engines do not fire except to make corrections in the path it is following. We say the ship is in free fall. So are the astronauts inside the ship, and everything else inside it.

The men are weightless. There is no down or up for them. They must fasten themselves down, otherwise they float in space. The slightest push

causes them to spin around. When they let go of a hammer, the tool floats free. If they give it a shove, the hammer moves in a straight line until it hits a wall of the cabin.

Liquids cannot be poured—there's no up or down. Liquids must be kept in containers, otherwise they float free as droplets. They must be squeezed out of tubes into the mouth of an astronaut, or into a container that has a cover on it.

Astronauts can't move around much inside a spaceship, but they exercise a lot. They go to sleep for several hours, eat concentrated foods at regular intervals, exercise between meals, make observations, take pictures of the earth and stars, and report by radio to the earth.

When an astronaut has to urinate he uses a plastic bag. Valves on the bag control flow into it, and also out. The urine is expelled outside the ship and into space. Occasionally small samples are held in plastic bottles and brought back to earth for analysis by doctors. Bowel movements are sealed in a similar manner. A bactericide is introduced into the bag to control decay and odor. The bags are stowed in a sewage storage area. The bags may be placed aboard vehicles that are left in space. Or some may be brought back to earth for analysis.

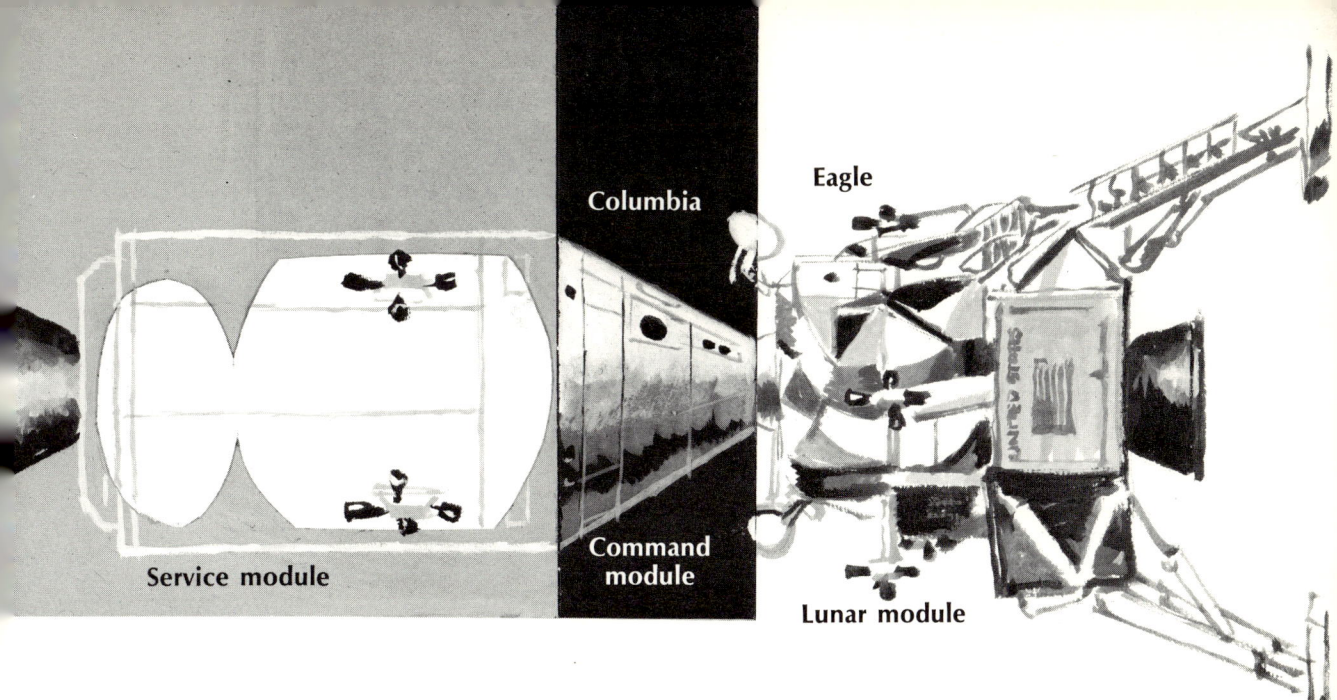

Scientists must have information about all aspects of the mission so they can improve equipment, and make future missions more effective.

When the coasting flight of Apollo 11 began, the command module sat atop the service module. The command module was called Columbia. The third part of the mission—the part that actually landed on the moon—was called the lunar module, or simply the LM (pronounced LEM). In the Apollo 11 flight the LM was given the code name of Eagle. In the early part of the mission the LM rode in the nose of the upper-stage rocket. Later on it was transferred to the nose of the command module. Here's how the transfer was made.

The command and service modules, which were fastened together and called the CSM, separated from the third-stage rocket that carried the Eagle in its nose, and turned about. Slowly, carefully, small rockets were fired to bring the combined modules to a soft docking with the LM. The ships eased together. Contact was made; the LM was pulled free of the rocket. The Columbia, with the LM on its nose, swung about. The third-stage engines were fired briefly to put the casing in an orbit that would not interfere with the modules. When they were ready, the astronauts could crawl out of the Columbia and into the Eagle.

The path of the ship to the moon was checked continually. Small rocket engines on the service module were fired to make corrections. As the hours went by, the speed of the ship got slower and slower—the gravity of the earth acted as a brake. It pulled on the ship, causing it to lose speed. When the ship was about 43,000 miles from the moon, it entered a region where the pull of the moon's gravity was stronger than the pull of the earth's gravity. The ship went faster and faster, all the while moving closer and closer to the moon.

If nothing were done the ship would have sped beyond the moon. Now the ship was flipped over so the service-module engines pointed forward. The engines were fired and the ship slowed down. The moon's gravity held the ship in orbit 70 miles above the surface. The astronauts could see details of the lunar surface. Preparations for the lunar landing moved ahead rapidly.

The hatch aboard Apollo 11 connecting Columbia and Eagle was opened. The environment in the LM was measured to be sure it was the same as that in the command module. Then Colonel Edwin E. Aldrin, Jr., and Neil A. Armstrong crawled through the yard-wide hatch from the command module to the LM. The hatch was closed tightly

and the docking collar was removed, leaving Lt. Colonel Michael Collins alone inside the command module.

Eagle separated from the mother ship. Small jets flipped it over so its engine was frontward. The engine fired, Eagle slowed down and went into a new orbit. Meanwhile Columbia, commanded by Astronaut Michael Collins, maintained altitude and continued in its path around the moon.

The LM is really the first spaceship ever made. All other ships that have traveled in space had to be smooth and streamlined because they had to come back to earth through the atmosphere. The LM is designed to travel only where there is no atmosphere, and to land on the moon where gravity is only one-sixth of earth's gravity. The LM would not be strong enough to support itself and the men inside if it were exposed to earth's gravity.

The ship looks like a gigantic bug with antennas sprouting from the surface, and four long spiderlike legs. In fact, it is often called "the bug," or "the spider." But it's a big one; for the LM weighs 16 tons and stands 23 feet tall. That's about the height of a two-story house.

The LM is made of millions of parts. But it can

be divided into two main sections. One is the descent stage. It contains the engines to lower the entire ship onto the lunar surface. The other section is the ascent stage. It is the upper part of the LM, and the only part of the ship that leaves the surface of the moon. The lower section, the descent stage, stays on the moon. It becomes the launching platform for the upper section.

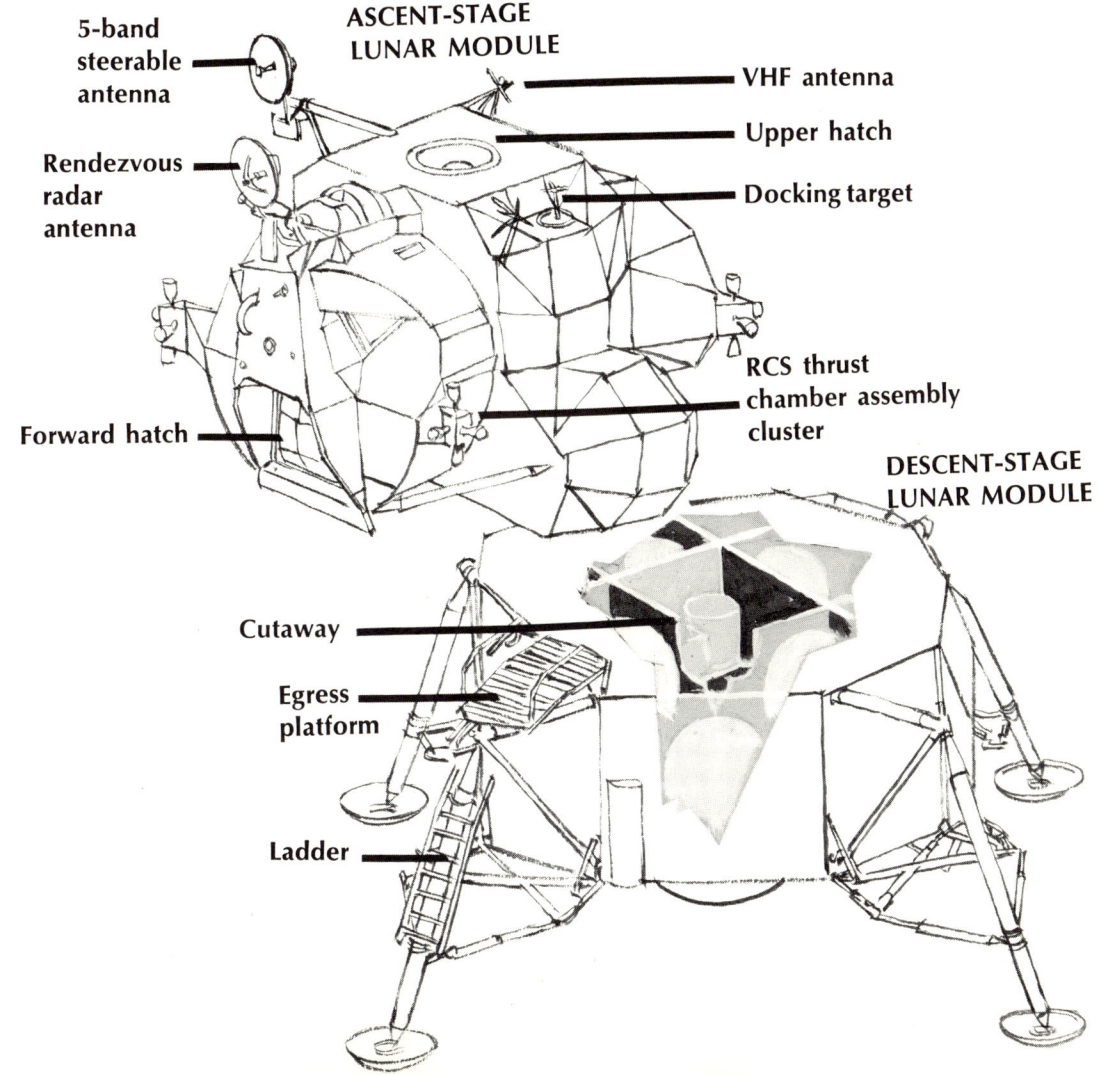

The cabin of the ship is a cylinder 7 feet in diameter. The walls are thick because several layers of insulating material are packed into the spaces between the inner and outer walls. The LM takes about one hour to travel from lunar orbit to the surface of the moon. During that time it is exposed to temperatures that may be as low as 400 degrees below zero, and as high as 250 degrees above zero. The temperature in the cabin must be maintained close to 70 degrees, so there is need for very good insulation.

There are no seats or hammocks in the cabin and so a lot of weight is saved. The astronauts decided that seats are not needed for several reasons. Landing on the moon is fairly gentle and so a seat is not needed for shock absorption. The landing operation takes only about one hour, and the astronauts felt that they could stand for that short period. They are supported by harnesses that hold them loosely and so prevent floating in space. During sleep periods, after landing on the moon, the astronauts lie on the flat floor of the LM.

When the LM of Apollo 11 first made separation from the mother ship it still moved in orbit around the moon. But the orbit was one that

brought it in closer to the surface. Slow-down rockets changed the orbit during descent. When Eagle was 50,000 feet above the lunar surface, the astronauts received the go-ahead from Mission Control: "You are go for PDI" (powered descent insertion). The engines were turned on full. For 12 minutes they burned, not stopping until Eagle was only 5 feet above the Sea of Tranquillity. The astronauts watched the altitude indicators to be sure the ship was on an even keel. Slowly the LM settled down. Great clouds of dust were blown up by the blast of the engines, and the heat melted surface rock. Cords that hung from the saucerlike feet sensed the surface—the engines cut off and all four "feet" were in contact. As the weight of the ship pushed on them, the legs telescoped. They pushed against wafflelike aluminum sponges inside the legs to take up the shock.

Man had landed on the moon. The time was 4:17:41 P.M. (E.D.T.), the late afternoon of July 20, 1969. Immediately the astronauts wanted to get out of the ship and onto the moon. But all systems had to be checked first. Mission Control in Houston, Texas, had to see that all aspects of the flight, the condition of the ship and the men, were OK before a go-ahead could be given.

When all was clear Armstrong and Aldrin put on their helmets, boots, gloves, and backpacks. These are life-support units that contain all the equipment needed to keep a man alive. The backpack contains oxygen for breathing, a pack for removing water vapor from the air, chemicals for removing carbon dioxide, a system for circulating cold water through tubes to pick up body heat, radio transmitters and receivers and the batteries to power them. When an astronaut steps onto the moon there are no connections between him and

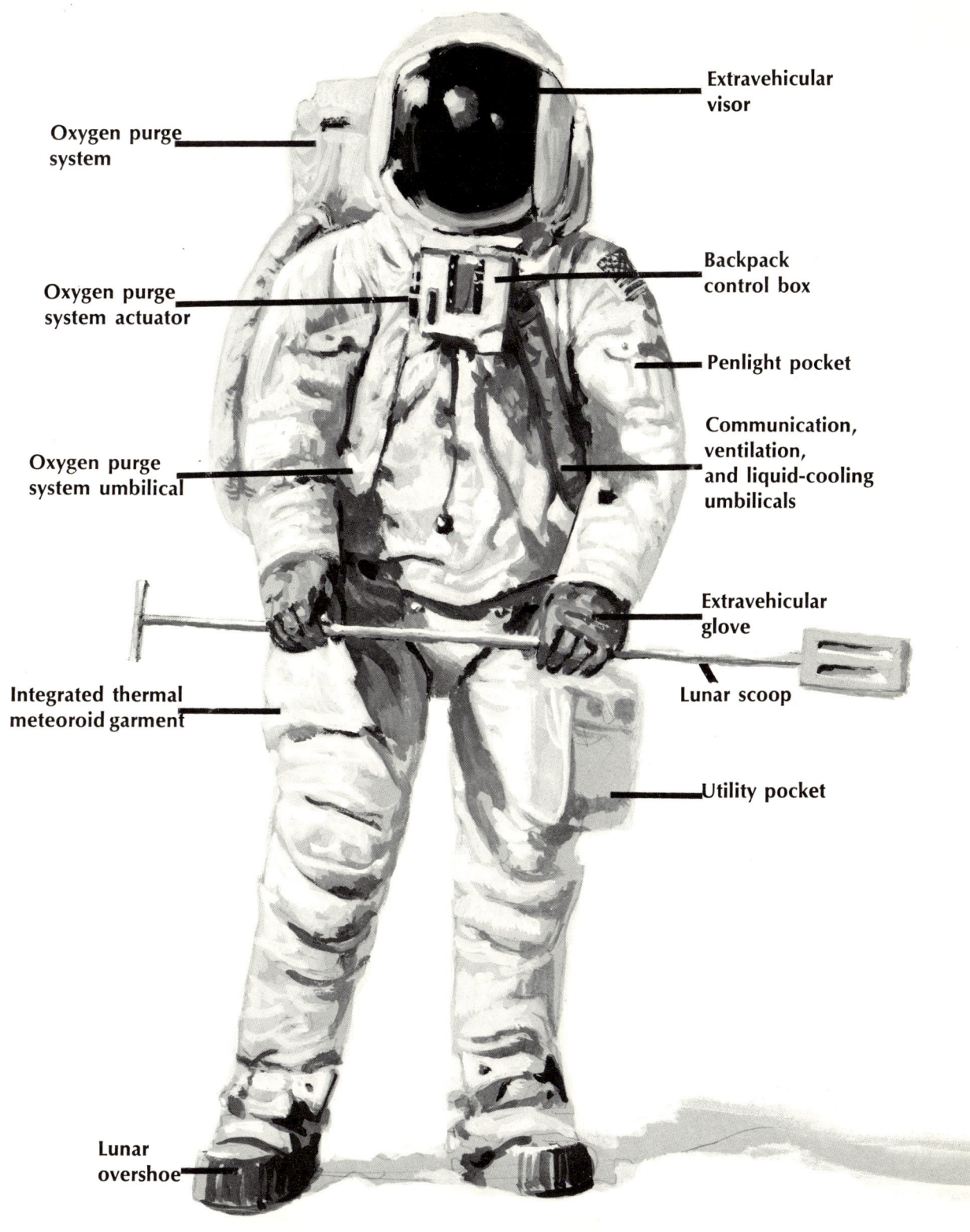

the LM. He relies completely on the backpack to keep himself alive.

Armstrong and Aldrin depressurized the cabin of Eagle. They opened the hatch. Armstrong lay on his stomach and wriggled backward out of the hatch. He crossed a porchlike platform and worked his way to the ladder. Eleven feet below him was the surface of the moon. With great care to be sure the suit did not snag or tear, he climbed down the ladder—one step at a time. At 10:56 P.M. (E.D.T.) on July 20, 1969, Astronaut Armstrong took his first step on the moon. As he made that historic step he said these historic words, "That's one small step for a man, one giant leap for mankind." At that moment man's dream of exploring another world firsthand came true. Armstrong looked around at the lunar scape. With a special tool he scooped up samples of lunar dust and rock, and put them into sacks for return to the LM.

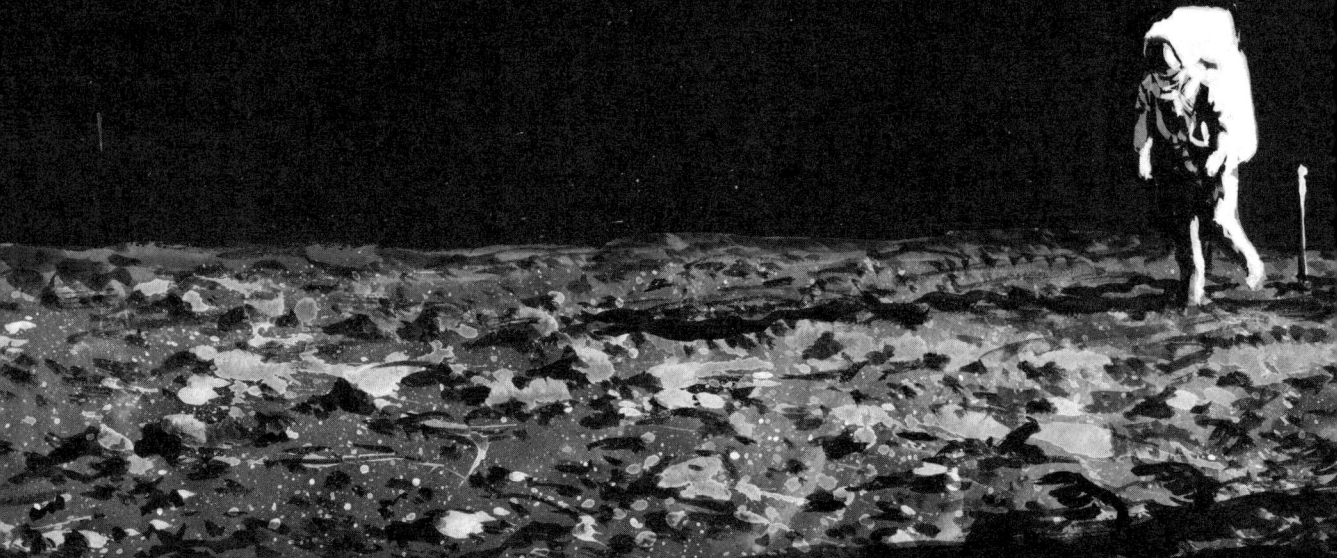

Within minutes Colonel Aldrin joined Armstrong. For two hours and fourteen minutes they walked, ran, and jumped on the lunar surface. All the time a TV camera was televising the event, sending historic pictures to receivers in California and from there to the entire world via satellite.

The astronauts returned to the Eagle. Climbing the ladder was easy as far as weight was concerned. The weights of the backpack and the space suit

did not bother them because of the low gravity of the moon. But all movements were awkward because of the restrictions of the suit. And the men had to move carefully to be certain the suit did not snag or rip.

All lunar samples were kept in closed containers. Biologists did not know what kind of organisms, if any, exist on the moon. Some of them might be dangerous to human beings. Lunar samples were not to be opened until they had been carefully checked to see their effects on test plants and animals at the Lunar Receiving Laboratory at the Manned Spacecraft Center in Houston, Texas.

Armstrong and Aldrin planted a flag of the United States in the Sea of Tranquillity. They left a plaque signed by the Apollo 11 astronauts and the President of the United States. Medals honoring the five men who have died while in the Russian and American space programs were also left on the moon. These remained along with the lunar experiment package.

The experiments included devices to measure the temperature of the moon's surface, to register any slight motions in the crust of the surface, to determine the presence of rare gases such as helium, argon, and krypton. Also, sensitive instruments to measure the strength and frequency of high-energy solar particles were placed there. Electricity generated by solar cells will keep the instruments working. The electricity also powers the radios that send the information back to the earth. The instruments are encased inside shiny, heat-reflecting covers. Unless they are hit by meteorites the instruments should continue to operate for three or four years. An assembly of bright mirrors to reflect laser beams sent from the earth was erected. The power supply and the instruments are together called ALSEP—the Apollo Lunar Surface Experiment Package.

Twenty-one hours after the landing, preparations were made for return to the command module. The astronauts stowed all gear and samples, and ate a good meal. Equipment no longer needed, such as boots, gloves, and backpacks, was left behind. They checked with Mission Control to be sure all their readings were go; and they checked with Michael Collins, the CSM pilot, to be sure he was ready for the docking maneuver. The upper stage of the Eagle, weighing 5 tons, was ready to rendezvous with Columbia.

The ascent-stage engines, the ones in the upper part of the LM, were fired. Just before lift-off, connection between the ascent and descent stages was broken. The ascent stage rose on a pillar of flame; silently, because the airless moon is a soundless world. The descent stage served as a launching platform. It remained on the surface of the moon.

The LM rose steadily, heeled over, and pursued the CSM which was circling the moon at a height of 70 miles. Meanwhile Michael Collins in the CSM had replaced the docking collar in the nose of the command module.

The LM pilot fired his engines sparingly, ever mindful of the need to conserve fuel. Slowly, the LM overtook the command module. As he neared the ship, Armstrong lined himself up with an illuminated marker on the CSM. Slowly the ships came together. Eagle was locked, held securely in the docking collar of Columbia.

Astronauts Armstrong and Aldrin moved through the connecting tube from the LM to the command module. Dust and rock samples from the moon were transferred from Eagle to Columbia.

The LM was detached, left to orbit the moon, and ultimately to crash into the surface when its orbit decayed.

The docking collar was jettisoned, hatches were battened down securely, and Columbia was ready to return to earth. Mission Control advised the astronauts how long it would be before the men at Houston sent a signal to start the engines in the service module. The astronauts fastened their belts and awaited the moment. The engines fired, accelerating the CSM, pushing it out of lunar orbit, and putting the vehicle in an orbit that would cause it to coast toward the earth.

The journey back to the earth took 59 hours

and 36 minutes. Engines aboard the service module were fired occasionally to correct the flight path. The CSM went faster and faster as earth's gravity pulled on it. It reached a speed of nearly 25,000 miles an hour. After the path of flight had been well established and corrected, the service module was no longer needed. It was separated from the command module. This occurred between 700 and 800 miles above the surface of the earth. Small thrust engines aboard the service module pushed it out of the path of the command module.

The command module was speeding freely toward the earth. Small engines swung the module about so the broad, blunt end, 12 feet across, was turned forward. The astronauts faced away from the direction in which they were moving.

When Columbia slammed into the atmosphere, the temperature on the leading side soared to 5,000 degrees—much hotter than the melting point of iron. Heavy insulation protected the astronauts from the heat. Indeed, much of the heat was carried off as layers of plastic peeled away from the ship. The front of the ship had a heat shield, made of layers of strong plastic that turned white hot and peeled away (ablated) as the temperature went up.

Twenty-five thousand feet above the earth small parachutes opened. These slowed and steadied the ship to keep it from swinging from side to side. Shortly after the chutes opened, the path of the module was almost straight downward. The descent was still very fast. Three small additional chutes were released. They pulled out the main parachutes, red and white striped and each measuring more than 80 feet across.

When these chutes opened, the speed of the module dropped sharply. At splashdown the speed was only 20 miles an hour.

Frogmen dropped from helicopters. They fastened a flotation collar to the module to keep it from sinking. The astronauts emerged. Man's first mission to another world was completed. As Neil Armstrong said: a giant leap for mankind had been made. The way was opened for further exploration of the moon.

In the years ahead more astronauts will go to the moon. New experiments will be set up on the lunar surface. Astronauts will spend a week or two on the moon, exploring the variety of lunar features

—the mountainous area, the lunar valleys and crevices, the rilles, deep and shallow craters.

Future Apollo missions will carry small jet-powered vehicles to the moon. Astronauts will ride in them to reach distant locations. Also Lunar Rovers will be carried to the moon. They will be tractorlike vehicles that will roam the surface of the moon. Astronauts will be able to see the entire surface firsthand.

Astronomers will build telescopes on the moon. With a small telescope on the moon they will be able to see more than astronomers can see from earth, using the largest telescopes available. And astronomers will build radio telescopes on the half of the moon that is always turned from the earth. Such telescopes will be able to "see" farther into space and to explore parts of the universe that so far man has been unable to probe.

But Apollo means more than that. In the years ahead men will explore firsthand the rest of the solar system, the stars, and even the galaxies that lie beyond our own. We shall look back at Apollo as a giant stride into space; the stride that finally broke man free of earth's mighty grip and opened the way to the stars.

MANNED SPACE FLIGHTS
Vostok I to Apollo II

SPACECRAFT	LAUNCH DATE	ASTRONAUT(S)	ORBITS	FLIGHT TIME	HIGHLIGHTS
Vostok 1 (U.S.S.R.)	Apr. 12, 1961	Yuri A. Gagarin	1	1 hr. 48 mins.	First manned flight.
Mercury-Redstone 3 (U.S.)	May 5, 1961	Alan B. Shepard, Jr.	Suborbital	0 hr. 15 mins.	First American in space.
Mercury-Redstone 4 (U.S.)	July 21, 1961	Virgil I. Grissom	Suborbital	0 hr. 16 mins.	Capsule sank.
Vostok 2 (U.S.S.R.)	Aug. 6, 1961	Gherman S. Titov	17	25 hrs. 18 mins.	More than 24 hours in space.
Mercury-Atlas 6 (U.S.)	Feb. 20, 1962	John H. Glenn, Jr.	3	4 hrs. 55 mins.	First American in orbit.
Mercury-Atlas 7 (U.S.)	May 24, 1962	M. Scott Carpenter	3	4 hrs. 56 mins.	Landed 250 miles from target.
Vostok 3 (U.S.S.R.)	Aug. 11, 1962	Andrian G. Nikolayev	64	94 hrs. 22 mins.	First group flight (Vostok 3 and 4).
Vostok 4 (U.S.S.R.)	Aug. 12, 1962	Pavel R. Popovich	48	70 hrs. 57 mins.	Came within 3.1 miles of Vostok 3 on first orbit.
Mercury-Atlas 8 (U.S.)	Oct. 3, 1962	Walter M. Schirra, Jr.	6	9 hrs. 13 mins.	Landed 5 miles from target.
Mercury-Atlas 9 (U.S.)	May 15, 1963	L. Gordon Cooper, Jr.	22	34 hrs. 20 mins.	First long U.S. flight.
Vostok 5 (U.S.S.R.)	June 14, 1963	Valery F. Bykovsky	81	119 hrs. 6 mins.	Second group flight (Vostok 5 and 6).

MANNED SPACE FLIGHTS (Cont.)

(U.S.S.R.)	Vostok 6	June 16, 1963	Valentina V. Tereshkova	48	70 hrs. 50 mins.	Passed within 3 miles of Vostok 5; first woman in space.
(U.S.S.R.)	Voskhod 1	Oct. 12, 1964	Vladimir M. Komarov Konstantin P. Feoktistov Dr. Boris B. Yegorov	16	24 hrs. 17 mins.	First 3-man craft.
(U.S.S.R.)	Voskhod 2	Mar. 18, 1965	Aleksei A. Leonov Pavel I. Belyayev	17	26 hrs. 2 mins.	First man outside spacecraft in 10-minute "walk" (Leonov).
(U.S.)	Gemini 3	Mar. 23, 1965	Virgil I. Grissom John W. Young	3	4 hrs. 53 mins.	First manned orbital maneuvers.
(U.S.)	Gemini 4	June 3, 1965	James A. McDivitt Edward H. White, 2nd	62	97 hrs. 48 mins.	21-minute "space walk" (White).
(U.S.)	Gemini 5	Aug. 21, 1965	L. Gordon Cooper, Jr. Charles Conrad, Jr.	120	190 hrs. 56 mins.	First extended manned flight.
(U.S.)	Gemini 7	Dec. 4, 1965	Frank Borman James A. Lovell, Jr.	206	330 hrs. 35 mins.	Longest space flight.
(U.S.)	Gemini 6-A	Dec. 15, 1965	Walter M. Schirra, Jr. Thomas P. Stafford	16	25 hrs. 52 mins.	Rendezvous within 1 foot of Gemini 7.
(U.S.)	Gemini 8	Mar. 16, 1966	Neil A. Armstrong David R. Scott	6.5	10 hrs. 42 mins.	First docking to Agena target.
(U.S.)	Gemini 9-A	June 3, 1966	Thomas P. Stafford Eugene A. Cernan	45	72 hrs. 21 mins.	Rendezvous; extravehicular activity; precision landing.
(U.S.)	Gemini 10	July 18, 1966	John W. Young Michael Collins	43	70 hrs. 47 mins.	Rendezvous with 2 targets; Agena package retrieved.
(U.S.)	Gemini 11	Sept. 12, 1966	Charles Conrad, Jr. Richard F. Gordon, Jr.	44	71 hrs. 17 mins.	Rendezvous and docking.
(U.S.)	Gemini 12	Nov. 11, 1966	James A. Lovell, Jr. Edwin E. Aldrin, Jr.	59	94 hrs. 33 mins.	3 successful extravehicular trips.

(U.S.S.R.)	Soyuz 1	Apr. 23, 1967	Vladimir M. Komarov	17	25 hrs. 12 mins.	Heaviest manned craft; crashed, killing Komarov.
(U.S.)	Apollo 7	Oct. 11, 1968	Walter M. Schirra, Jr. Donn F. Eisele R. Walter Cunningham	163	260 hrs. 9 mins.	First manned flight of Apollo spacecraft.
(U.S.S.R.)	Soyuz 3	Oct. 26, 1968	Georgi T. Beregovoy	64	95 hrs.	Rendezvous with unmanned Soyuz 2.
(U.S.)	Apollo 8	Dec. 21, 1968	Frank Borman James A. Lovell, Jr. William A. Anders	Moon orbital (10 orbits)	147 hrs.	First manned voyage around moon.
(U.S.S.R.)	Soyuz 4	Jan. 14, 1969	Vladimir A. Shatalov	48	71 hrs. 14 mins.	Docking of two craft in orbit; passage of cosmonauts between craft.
(U.S.S.R.)	Soyuz 5	Jan. 15, 1969	Boris Volynov Yevgeni Khrunov Alexei Yeliseyev	49	72 hrs. 46 mins.	
(U.S.)	Apollo 9	Mar. 3, 1969	James A. McDivitt Russell L. Schweickart David R. Scott	Earth orbital (151 orbits)	241 hrs. 1 min.	Docking of LM and CSM, first walk in space with self-contained life-support system.
(U.S.)	Apollo 10	May 18, 1969	Thomas P. Stafford Eugene A. Cernan John W. Young	Moon orbital (31 orbits)	192 hrs. 3 mins.	Descent to within 9 miles of lunar surface.
(U.S.)	Apollo 11	July 16, 1969	Neil A. Armstrong Edwin E. Aldrin, Jr. Michael Collins	Moon orbit for Columbia (31 orbits); time on moon: 21 hrs. 38 mins.	195 hrs. 18 mins.	Armstrong and Aldrin land Eagle on the moon; they walk on the moon.

INDEX

Aldrin, Edwin E., Jr., 1-2, 15-16, 28
   moon landing, 20, 22-23
Apollo 11, 1-2
   coasting of, 9-10, 13
   gravity and, 14-15
   launching, 8-9
   module transfers, 13-14, 26-28
   return to earth, 28-31
Apollo Lunar Surface Experiment Package (ALSEP), 25-26
argon, 25
Armstrong, Neil A., 1-2, 15-16, 28, 31
   moon landing, 20, 22-23
astronomy, 32
atmosphere re-entry, 30

backpacks, 20, 22, 23, 26

California, 23
Cape Kennedy, Florida, 2
clouds, 6
Collins, Michael, 2, 16, 26
Columbia, see command module (Columbia)
command module (Columbia), 9, 13-14
   Collins command, 2, 16, 26, 27
   lunar module departure from, 15, 16, 18-19
   lunar module return to, 26-28
   return journey of, 28-31
crew, 6-8
   command module activities of, 10, 12

command module re-entry, 26-28
   compartments for, 9, 10
   life-support equipment, 20, 22
   lunar landing, 1-2, 15-16, 18-20
   moon exploration, 22-26
   return to earth, 28-31
CSM (*see also* command module (Columbia); service module), 13-14, 26-29

dust, 6
   lunar, 2, 19, 22, 24, 28

Eagle, *see* lunar module (Eagle, LM)
earth, the:
   gravity of, 14, 16, 29
   human orbiting of, 7-8, 9
   satellite orbiting of, 2, 5-6
   spaceship return to, 28-31
electricity, 25-26

feet, of lunar module, 20
flag, 25
Florida, 2
frogmen, 30

Gagarin, Yuri A., 7
gases, 25
Glenn, John H., Jr., 7-8

helium, 25
Houston, Texas, 10, 20, 24, 28

(36)

instruments, 6, 25-26

krypton, 25

laser beams, 26
life-support equipment, 20, 22
liquids, in weightlessness, 12
living organisms, 24
lunar module (Eagle, LM), 1, 13-14
   command module departure, 15, 16, 18-19
   command module return, 26-28
   design of, 16-18, 20
   landing operation of, 18-20, 22
Lunar Receiving Laboratory, Houston, 24
Lunar Rovers, 32

Manned Spacecraft Center, Houston, 10, 24
   Mission Control in, 19, 20, 26, 28
maps, 6
Mare Tranquillitatis, *see* Sea of Tranquillity
measurement, instruments for, 6, 25-26
medals, 25
Mercury (orbiting capsule), 7-8
mirrors, 26
Mission Control, 19, 20, 26, 28
moon, the, 1-2, 4-5
   experiment pack on, 25-26
   exploration plans, 31-32
   first visit, 22-26
   gravity of, 14-15, 16, 24
   landing operation on, 18-20
   launching for return from, 17, 27

oxygen, 10, 20

parachutes, 30
Presidential plaque, 25
Project Apollo, 2, 7, 31-32

radiation, 6
radio, 10, 20, 26
radio telescopes, 32
rockets, 5, 7
   module transfer and, 13-14
   Saturn launching, 2, 8-9
rocks, 20
   sample collection, 2, 22, 24, 28
Russia, 7, 8, 25

satellites, 2, 5-6
Saturn 5 rocket, 2, 8-9
Sea of Tranquillity, 1, 2, 19, 25
service module, 9, 10, 13-14, 29
solar particles, 25
sound, 27
space suits, 22, 23-24
Sputnik 1, 5

telescopes, 32
television, 6
   landing broadcast, 23
temperature, 18
   atmosphere re-entry, 30
   moon surface, 25
Tereshkova, Valentina V., 8
Texas, 10, 20, 24, 28
Tranquillity Base, 1

Union of Soviet Socialist Republics (Russia), 7, 8, 25
United States of America, 7-8, 25
urine bags, 12

Vostok 1, 7
Vostok 6, 8

weightlessness, 10, 12, 18, 23-24

ABOUT THE AUTHOR

Dr. Franklyn M. Branley is well known as the author of many excellent science books for young people of all ages. He is also co-editor of the Let's-Read-and-Find-Out science books.

Dr. Branley is Astronomer and Chairman of the American Museum–Hayden Planetarium in New York City.

He holds degrees from New York University, Columbia University, and the State University of New York College at New Paltz. He lives with his family in Woodcliff Lake, New Jersey.

ABOUT THE ILLUSTRATOR

Two days before Neil Armstrong set foot on the moon, Louis S. Glanzman, using his knowledge and imagination, drew that historic scene for the cover of a major national magazine. His interest in man's quest for the moon is evident.

Mr. Glanzman was raised in Virginia but moved to New York when he was thirteen. By the age of sixteen he had started work—he wrote and illustrated his own comic strip.

Now a well-known artist and illustrator of many books, Mr. Glanzman lives on Long Island with his wife and four daughters.

DISCARDED

```
629.45   Branley, Franklyn M
Bra
     Man in space to the
       moon
```

DISCARDED